D1163916

A NEW GUIDE TO ROLLEI PHOTOGRAPHY

A NEW GUIDE TO ROLLEI PHOTOGRAPHY

by Fritz Henle
with H. M. Kinzer

A Studio Book
THE VIKING PRESS
New York

Published in 1965 by The Viking Press, Inc.
625 Madison Avenue, New York, N.Y. 10022
Published simultaneously in Canada by
The Macmillan Company of Canada Limited
Library of Congress catalog card number: 65–12576
Printed in Germany

Acknowledgment
The text of this book is adapted from articles which first appeared in Popular Photography *and are used by their permission.*

CONTENTS

TO THE MEMORY OF LENI PREETORIUS

INTRODUCTION

Putting together a book intended to help its readers is a sober responsibility. The author's first instinct is to write the book for himself — to "get something off his chest," to put his conceptions and opinions into systematic order. In this effort, his audience sometimes gets lost. So the conscientious author must always try to see his own experience, somehow, through his readers' eyes, to discover what that experience can do for them.

This book is different from my previous books in both origin and organization. It grew from a series of monthly columns written for the world's largest photographic magazine over a period of two and a half years. The column, addressed to users of the Rolleiflex and other cameras of the same type, drew an impressive volume of mail, about equally divided between thanks for a past item and suggestions for future ones.

This made the feature essentially self-generating, so that I was continually sure of dealing with subjects of genuine interest to the readers. Sometimes a subject — such as the photographing of children — elicited so much response that I found it necessary (and pleasant) to do another column on the same subject, answering questions or supplying information that had not been covered the first time.

Since I have said that the author of a book like this one should not use it as a soap-box for his personal views, perhaps I should make a small but important exception. One thing has bothered me for a long time, perhaps more than it should: people who use the twin-lens reflex so often do so because "it's a tremendous camera, in spite of the square pictures it makes." They go so far as to say that, right from the beginning, they plan whether a shot will crop to a vertical or a horizontal — the presumption being that the natural format is out of the question.

For years, I have waged a small private war in defense of the square format, as the reader of this book will note from repeated references. It went so far that finally, in response to some letters, I was forced to write a column denying that I was "against" verticals and horizontals! The fact is simply that I find a natural harmony in the square, and more often than not I am able to *add* to a picture, rather than detract from it, by keeping to the square. I don't think this is any particular gift of mine; anybody can learn to do it.

There is another "personal crusade" being carried on in these pages, though it is not so explicitly stated. This is the fight against deadly seriousness in technical

matters, which kills the pleasure of photography. I don't mean only for amateurs (whose only motivations in picture-taking are pleasure and self-fulfillment), but for professionals as well. It is almost a cliché in our society that the work you do for a living is something you don't enjoy — or even something you hate. To whatever extent this is true, I am one of the fortunate few who completely enjoy their work. This has been true not only since my first success, but all during the period when I was working toward it. I can't imagine photography being a dull, grinding occupation. So it certainly cannot be a dull avocation. Yet I have watched amateurs go from fascination to tedium in a few months, when they were led to believe they couldn't enjoy photography without doing their own processing, or endlessly testing the resolving power of lenses, or pitting one speedlight unit against another, or mastering the organic chemistry of film development.

Photography is a pleasure. If it weren't, I wouldn't be in it. It should be a to you. This book is put together to augment that pleasure. You can read it a page at a time, or straight through at one sitting.

My only regret in preparing the articles for magazine publication has been that space permitted using only one small picture each time. Here we have abundantly remedied this problem by supplementing each piece with an additional full-page photograph, and adding a generous supplement of pictures.

By agreement with *Popular Photography*, all the texts have been adapted for publication; often they have been expanded for greater usefulness in a permanent volume.

Fritz Henle

THE AUTHOR in a portrait by Peter Schults. I offer it with some embarrassment; the publisher insisted I must let all my old—and new—friends know what I look like. As for technical information: most of the pictures in this book were made on Kodak Ektachrome Professional, Kodak Tri-X, or Perutz 21 or 27 films. Processing of the color was done by Studio 13 in Zurich, the black-and-white by Motal Custom Darkrooms in New York. I have endeavored to give pertinent details and observations with each photograph.

What's Wrong with a Square?

I am continually surprised to find that there are still people in photography who think there is something basically wrong with a square-format picture. Some buyers of twin-lens reflexes today think of the square frame as simply a convenient way to take both verticals and horizontals without turning the camera. Most of the time these people are just wasting about one third of their picture area needlessly.

Certainly, most of the pictures we see are either verticals or horizontals. This is probably because the first cameras were designed by conservative people to conform to the proportions of the paintings of that day; photography then was conceived to be a kind of extension of art as it existed. Of course, masterpieces had been painted for centuries in a square format—but not *most* masterpieces.

I haven't always been a square-format photographer. I learned my trade behind an 8×10 view camera, and had already learned to compose on its groundglass before I saw my first Rolleiflex in a store window three decades ago. It never occurred to me that the square picture would be a drawback. I thought of it instead as a horizontal extension of a vertical picture, and a vertical extension of a horizontal—that is, as an addition to, not a subtraction from the picture.

Ever since then I have seen the square format in this way. But at the same time, this view has not been dogmatic. A lot of my pictures, naturally, are verticals and horizontals, because the subject matter demands it. Let me put it this way: when I photograph a tree—an obviously vertical subject—I study its relationship with its surroundings to make sure the "vertical" concept isn't robbing me of some elements that might make the picture better and stronger. As often as not, I end by making a more-or-less square picture in which the tree still dominates with its vertical lines. The same would be true of a horizontal subject like a skyline or a parade.

It seems to me now that the prejudice against squareness has just about been overcome. Seldom do I hear a client ask me to crop a square picture, when I have given some thought to composing it in the groundglass.

Most manufacturers of twin-lens reflexes put crossed lines on the groundglass to indicate the conventional proportion of vertical and horizontal pictures, and some photographers seem to take these as limitations. I have even heard one say that he tried to use only the small square formed by the crossing of the four lines, just to make sure he wouldn't miss any part of the picture! Of course, one great virtue of this type of camera is that the groundglass shows exactly what you're getting (barring the possibility of parallax), and you should be training your eye to look into every corner of that frame, and along every edge, so that you will know what the picture contains the instant the shutter clicks. Nothing is more the mark of a novice than his frequent discovery of whole elements in a print that he hadn't seen when he made the shot.

Of course, there are instances in which you can't use the whole square area for the kind of pictures you want; for example, when you can't get close enough to the subject. But when this happens to me and I must crop, I am grateful for the relatively large negative size so the necessary degree of enlargement will require no sacrifice of quality.

NETS surround us, more or less tightly, in life as well as in the search for pictures. Above all, wherever there is water, they furnish a good frame — or, as here in Dubrovnik, a good drapery. Nets veil what is distracting, reveal what we want to show. This is a black-and-white print from an Ektachrome Professional transparency; 1/30 second, f/22.

More about Squareness

One of the continuing controversies about twin-lens reflexes is the question of the square format. My first magazine column was on that subject, and most of the mail about it since has been in agreement that the square *in itself* is a perfectly fine format for a great proportion of the pictures we take. Some readers say that more often than not they crop one side, top, or bottom, but they are glad to have the choice on the contact sheet.

I have a letter from a Texas man who sells pictures to national magazines, and whose work regularly appears in Central Texas newspapers. He says, "My editors like my pictures square. If they need a three-column shot, I make a 6×6-inch print; if it's a four-column, I make an 8×8-inch." I don't know what special considerations may make those Texas editors ask for square pictures, but it may be the same unexplained feeling that many of us have—that the square is generally a good shape for a photograph.

The Texan goes on to say that he "apparently" crops and composes his pictures in the groundglass, and that therefore something is lost if they are turned into verticals or horizontals later. He's no fanatic about twin-lens either and turns to 35-mm rangefinder, single-lens reflex, and 4×5 when special problems are presented.

Now, it's perfectly plain that if you want a full-length shot of a man, with nothing else in the picture, you'll choose a vertical; for a racing sports car, a horizontal. But very often the picture can be improved, can convey more information, if you can contrive to include some of the surroundings. This is where the square format serves best.

As I have made clear before, I don't think the square is the best format for every picture. There are two cases to be considered: one in which the composition is basically round or square, and which should be cropped square even if it's shot on 35-mm; another in which the subject is horizontal or vertical but the picture can be enriched by inclusion of props, patterns, or vistas at top, bottom, or sides to make a square.

These are things to think of while you're looking in the groundglass. The whole idea is to make the picture with the camera—not to reconstruct it out of afterthoughts.

CARIBBEAN SCHOONER near St. Croix, one of the U.S. Virgin Islands — my home. The dramatic effect comes from use of Gevaert Infrared film, which alters the black and white values. Such a subject lends itself to a variety of croppings from the original format.

When to Depart from the Square

To a twin-lens user it seems only logical to make most effective use of *all* the film exposed in each shot. Avoidance of cropping always leads to better quality, because a lesser degree of enlargement is necessary. Beyond that, when one is seriously committed to a square-format camera, he finds himself continually learning how to use all the frame—and not with trivial details, either.

When is it wise, then, to make nonsquare pictures with the twin-lens? First, of course, there are the times when all the eye training in the world can't help you really use the square to your satisfaction: the cloudless sky that no amount of filtration can make interesting: the intrusive tangle of underbrush, or group of people's heads, that won't fall into place in the composition.

Even more significantly, there are pictures whose dominant lines seem to fight the square's limitations. It might be a tall tower, with nothing nearby to balance it with a horizontal mass, which could be best treated as a dramatic, narrow vertical. It could be a landscape in which strength is dissipated by a bald sky and featureless foreground. The illustration I have chosen for this point—the Italian drummer—seemed to demand the vertical format.

Perhaps all this discussion of what belongs in a picture and what does not sounds theoretical or dogmatic. Let me assure you that I'm not setting down any rules; I believe that new rules are made every time we approach a new situation, and that your best guide is intuition—and a sharp eye.

I have done a lot of work with the Plaubel Veriwide camera, an instrument that is guaranteed to stretch anyone's vision into wide horizontals. But it is so different from the twin-lens in its way of seeing that its lessons can hardly be applied. What we're discussing here is the garden-variety horizontal or vertical, conceived in basically the same way as the square.

Sometimes it is wise to use the vertical for a portrait. I like to include some element other than head and shoulders, so the composition naturally falls into a square. But if a simple, unadorned portrait is wanted—like the conventional studio or newspaper wedding picture—then the vertical is a natural choice.

In those last few lines, I believe I have come close to the truth of this matter of format: the phrase "some other element." What we learn from the twin-lens discipline is that values can be *added* to the picture by filling the square. We can think of the horizontal and vertical as squares to which something has been *added* at the sides or top and bottom.

DRUMMER IN SIENA, ITALY. A painting-like quality gives the look of the Middle Ages to this traditional figure. The vertical cropping from the square seems to let the subject "grow."

Down Where Children Live

A lot of the arguments for and against various types of cameras, I know, are based on subjective feelings, and shouldn't be put forth as "facts." When it comes right down to cases, I'd be forced to say that I use a twin-lens reflex because I like to use a twin-lens reflex—and that's all there is to it. I've given fair trial to everything else, including the extremes of 35-mm and 11×14 view camera, and here I am back where I "found a home" three decades ago.

I begin with this because there is one often-mentioned advantage of the twin-lens that I feel goes beyond subjective—one that I think most people will concede. It has to do with the point of view that comes naturally from handling this type of camera. In normal use of the twin-lens, you are looking downward into a groundglass, which is transmitting an image of what is opposite the viewing lens, usually at the level of your chest, or lower.

This suggests that the twin-lens reflex is the ideal camera for looking head-on at subjects of somewhat less than adult height—children, for example. I think I can argue this point without seeming to limit this type of camera to smaller-than-adult subjects. It does seem obvious that when a camera is used as the direct extension of the eye of a six-foot human being, it's going to be looking down upon three-foot human beings. And a lot of pictures I see bear this out; the kids seem always to be looking upward to some superior figure. We accept this, because that's the way we generally see children anyway. But maybe it's fairer to the child to take his picture from the viewpoint of another child.

I can anticipate the objections of my 35-mm friends; they will send me endless worm's-eye views of little tots made with miniature cameras whose owners sprawled on the turf to get them. I can also stand on a ladder and get pictures of the tops of children's heads with my reflex. It's simply a matter of the normal way of handling the camera.

In all seriousness, I feel that when I approach a child or a group of children with a twin-lens reflex, I am more a member of their group than I would be with another camera, and thus better able to reflect their world without distracting them, and without condescension. The very psychological effect of my bending forward to look into the groundglass is a kind of symbolic lowering of my physical advantage over them.

Let me offer a couple of examples of the way this has worked out in terms of finished pictures. Some time ago I photographed a young people's orchestra during a rehearsal. These were not little children, but they were seated, so this brought their heads a little above my own waist level. The best pictures from that group seemed to have been made from the chair of another musician seated among them. There was no self-consciousness, no looking down on the subject.

On another occasion, I saw my little daughter discovering the scent of a flower for the first time one day when I didn't have my camera with me. I knew I could never re-create that moment artificially, but I also knew that a moment like it would happen again. So on another day when I saw her investigating the flowers, I made sure to have the camera, and stooped alongside her so that it became a natural participant in the situation. I got a picture as fine as I could have hoped to get if I'd had the camera the first time.

LITTLE ST. CROIX BEAUTY. I went down to the child's level, from where the outside world seems so big, and the child seems perfectly natural. Notice, no toys, no "look-at-the-birdie." My lens exchanged glances with the child. 1/60 second, f/11.

Children Again

One of the first subjects I wrote about in my magazine column was taking children's pictures, and how the twin-lens is especially adapted for this kind of photography that so many people like to do. Judging from the mail I got, children are still the world's most photographed subjects. And I find that they are a never-ceasing challenge and fascination for my own camera. In fact, in my Virgin Islands home town, I have become something of an unofficial child photographer.

My first column on the subject pointed out how the natural shooting position of the twin-lens put it more or less on the child's level, so the pictures would not have the "condescending" look—always shot from the adult viewpoint. I also felt that the reflex was more of an object of curiosity, and less forbidding, than a camera which must be held tight against the face. Of course, these are subjective matters, and your own way of working has a lot to do with the way the camera is received as a "welcome guest" and with the way it looks at its small subjects.

Recently I have found the longer-focus lens of the Tele-Rollei especially useful for children, and use it almost exclusively for this kind of picture. It is the 135-mm Sonnar *f*/4, and of course there is a matching viewing lens.

With this focal length I can work a few feet farther away from the child, which is a distinct advantage when I want him to be unaware of what I'm doing. And because I am farther from the subject—still keeping the same image size—there is less chance of distorting any part of the body that extends toward the camera.

It is also an ideal focal length for getting head-and-shoulders shots without intimidating the child by moving the camera very close. Without supplementary lenses, it will not focus closer than about 8½ feet; with the Rolleinar close-up lens designated "0.35" it will work at from 5 to 8 feet, and if you should want to get closer (though probably not for children) the "0.7" Rolleinar works as close as 40 inches.

I am sometimes asked whether I make faces or play tricks to divert a child and get animated expressions. I am not able to do this, and actually it seems absurd that anyone should have to resort to it. After all, it is the photographer's real personality which should win the child's respect and cooperation. I do sometimes "stalk" the child, trying to remain unnoticed as long as possible, because there are some aspects of children's secret world that can never be shared consciously with the camera.

But then, even when the child realizes the camera is there, it need not break the spell. With a little practice, the twin-lens can be operated at some distance from the eye—hip level, for instance. You can prefocus with assurance if you stop down the lens as far as a motion-stopping shutter speed will let you. This means you need the groundglass only for viewfinding, so your eye doesn't need to be close to the hood.

The quality of light is of key importance in any photograph. With children, the main thing is to keep direct sun off the face. This means usually open shade, overcast, backlighting, or some other situation in which the sun is prevented from striking the face.

Periods of overcast are rather rare and short in my part of the world, so I must usually rely on one of the other ways of subduing the sun. Actually, I find that it is good to have direct sun in some part of the picture—even falling across some part of the child's figure—because it heightens contrast and lends strength to the composition. But be sure to keep it out of those little eyes!

Pages 20-21:
SUSANNE ON THE SWING. An upside-down picture, in which you "feel" the swing without seeing it. A picture of swinging — not of the swing! Try turning the picture upside down. Tele-Rollei, 1/125 second, f/11.

DUTCH GIRLS from the island of Marken. Even this young, they are full of sober tradition.

Page 22:
MEXICAN GIRL among the cactus. She is already a solicitous "mother," and far freer from illusion than her sisters in other countries. Life, like the cactus, has its thorns.

Page 23:
MY DAUGHTER TINA. Palms, sun, and the easy calm of St. Croix. In open shade, 1/60 second, f/16.

Other People's Babies

There's one set of problems to contend with in photographing children from, say, three or four into the teens, and quite another for working with infants. I've written a couple of times about the first category, but have never touched on the photography of the very young. I had occasion to think about the difference when some friends commissioned me to take pictures of their six-month-old daughter.

I had, of course, photographed my own children beginning at the age of one hour, but I had done it as a father rather than as a professional picture-taker. This request from "outside" made me think objectively as I would on any assignment.

The psychological difference between babies and older children, it seems to me, is that with the older ones the photographer has many more avenues of communication and resources for gaining response and cooperation. You can't address them as adults, with what grownups consider "rational" explanations and arguments, but you do have the whole range of language to use with whatever skill you possess. But before a child's vocabulary has gone beyond "mama" and a few other sounds associated with likes or dislikes, you must use other ways of getting responses—and you must be patient and unruffled when you fail to get them, or all is lost.

With a child so small, it is necessary to have the mother (or a competent baby-sitter) in attendance. Your attention is demanded by the image in the groundglass, and little creepers can run into trouble without your realizing it.

The attention span of a baby (as the psychologists call it) is brief, but varies considerably with individuals. The important thing is to halt the shooting as soon as the child grows impatient.

Light—both quantity and quality—is of great importance in photographing the very young. Strong lighting, either sun or artifical, is out of the question. Apart from the squinting and harsh shadows it causes, it can harm the eyes.

At the same time, I don't like to work where the light is inadequate if it can be avoided. Neither extremely wide apertures nor very slow shutter speeds are desirable for this kind of work; you need reasonable depth of field because you will be moving with the camera to frame the subject, and you need all the shutter speed you can manage to catch fleeting expressions and flailing arms and legs.

All this means that the light should be bright but not direct. In the Caribbean, where I spend much of my time, this usually means open shade, since the sky is seldom overcast. I am usually able to shoot at 1/250 second at around *f*/11, using conservatively rated Tri-X in open shade. (This is not an exposure recommendation. Sunlight varies so much that you should always rely on a meter or experience.)

I've kept for the end our customary little sermon about the special adaptability of the twin-lens to a particular kind of photography. What I have said before about its natural suitability to children is even more applicable to the very young: the twin-lens shooting position is about two feet lower than that of the 35-mm, so a lower vantage point is that much easier to reach.

With babies, I find too that the separation of eye from lens gives the little subject two points of interest to choose between. In my small example, the child has momentarily looked up at me, ignoring the camera itself.

MARGUERITE AND MARIA, in our garden at Millwood, N.Y. An attempt to capture the timeless mother-and-child theme. The picture says: they belong together, even when their eyes look elsewhere.

Shooting Pictures Sideways

The twin-lens is the ideal camera for what used to be called "candid" pictures of people—shots made without their being aware of the camera. This is because you look downward into its groundglass, and not directly at the subject, as with the rangefinder-viewfinder type. In addition, the twin-lens lends itself easily to sidewise aiming—that is, turning the lens to left or right to focus on the subject while still facing forward. This makes most subjects think you're just tinkering with the camera, not shooting.

This is a trick that some timid souls find absolutely indispensable when photographing strangers, because they're afraid of being attacked or cursed if their subject is aware of them. And even experienced pros have occasion to work this way once in a while—for instance, to catch a fleeting expression or an unself-conscious gesture.

I think it is important and valuable to show rapport between subject and photographer whenever possible. The best portraits—formal and informal—have this quality. And (by the way) the twin-lens has another advantage for portraiture: the subject can play to either the lens or the photographer, lending variety and change of pace to a sitting. With an eye-level camera, the subject has little choice but to look into the camera, unless directed otherwise.

But in grab-shooting and off-guard photography the object is to catch the very *absence* of rapport, the expression and gesture that grow in complete unawareness of the camera and the photographer. We work this way when the pose or action is such that the subject could not possibly repeat it or create it consciously. Some people deliberately shoot this way to embarrass the subject or to show him in a bad light; this is simply bad taste. The only excuse for off-guard photography is that it can reveal a hidden side of the subject, make him seem more responsive than otherwise.

The approach to off-guard shooting is different in one important way from that which involves the cooperation of the subject. You must be completely casual in the situation, reserving all your intense concentration for the image in the groundglass. Since you can't study the subject directly without attracting his attention, your only link with him is through the angled mirror behind your viewing lens.

If you're used to planning your picture by first looking at the subject, then translating the image onto the groundglass, it will take some practice to start from scratch with the groundglass. Watch for peaks of action and animation; back off far enough to be sure you're not cutting anything out. Work first with friends and family members; you'll be more at ease, and there will be less at stake if you fumble and betray your technique.

It's easiest to pretend to be fiddling with the camera if it's resting on some support, like a park bench, picnic table, or a piece of masonry. If you can sit down, balance it in your lap as you pretend to examine it. But right-angle grab-shooting on the run isn't impossible, through you must work quickly and be sure to use a shutter speed fast enough to arrest both your own motion and that of the subject.

I've heard of one photographer who goes to the trouble of fixing a black cardboard tube tightly around the focusing knob, so that the knob turns with the tube. He aims this cardboard "lens" at an imaginary subject, focusing by turning the tube, while the real lenses are turned on the subject and he is zeroing in on it on the groundglass. I've never gone quite this far, but it illustrates the ingenuity stimulated by the desire for off-guard pictures.

This kind of tricky right-angle picture-taking isn't limited to us twin-lensers, of course. There are right-angle viewfinders available for other camera types, usually fitting the accessory shoe. We just happen to be one jump ahead with our right-angle accessory built right in!

OLD SARDINIAN. This is just how I found him, so unnoticed, so "Wagnerian," so intensely devoted to doing nothing — a study in the sun of Sardinia.

XIII · PONT · MAX · OPVS

FOUNTAIN OF TREVI (left), perhaps the best-known one in Rome. But I was amused by the twin blacknesses of the monks in front of the twin whitenesses of the columns. Sun, water, stones, and religious garb — all unchanged through the centuries in Rome.

TUILERIES GARDENS (below), famous Paris meeting place, where the game of love and life still goes on as it did before the Revolution. In Paris, as in Rome, the photographer is least noticed from behind.

Natural Nudes

Nearly every photographer wants to try nudes at one time or another. Many never get around to it because the obstacles—getting a model and working with her successfully—seem too formidable. Some make the attempt but fail miserably, even though they are otherwise competent photographers. I knows some top pros who are unable to photograph the human figure without making it look like either a plaster cast or a subject for a French postcard.

Most of the difficulty lies in the model-photographer relationship, and not in photographic technique. If either or both are inhibited by the situation, or sense an unreality about it, failure is guaranteed.

I cannot advise you about finding a model. But it has been my experience that non-professionals are often better than those for whom posing is an everyday job. It is also true that a good figure model (good figure *plus* good working relationship) is a rarity. It would be an advantage for photographer and model to look at some examples of nudes together before the shooting session, so that they agree in general as to what is graceful, natural, and in good taste. Above all, a clear distinction must be made between "cheesecake" and the nude. If you are interested in the former, I'm afraid you will have to look elsewhere for advice.

When it comes to actual working with the model, especially if she is not experienced, you may find that the right-angle viewing and focusing of the twin-lens reflex is a distinct advantage. It fosters and preserves a kind of indirectness or impersonality; by its unobtrusiveness it encourages the model to take natural and unself-conscious poses. (The direct viewfinder is symbolically allied by some psychologists with the photographer's alleged "latent Peeping-Tomism." I don't necessarily agree with this.) To be more specific about this: when I am looking downward into the groundglass, rather than directly at the model, there is a kind of unspoken understanding that I am attending to my business, and the model can *feel* "unobserved" even though she *knows* otherwise.

As a setting for nudes, I would always choose something simple. Nature is the ideal background, and a beach or rocky waterfront situation is likely to be uncluttered. I would not introduce any props or other elements not found in the location: if I use a chair on the beach, it is because I have found one washed up by the tide.

When I cannot work outdoors, I will try to simulate daylight by the use of floods in an all-white studio. Generally the effect will be that of an overcast sky, since I prefer bouncelight to direct, harsh floodlighting. Of course, I use as much natural window daylight as possible.

In the accompanying picture, the attempt was to make the figure seem an inseparable part of its surroundings, and to compare and contrast the textures and tonalities of flesh and stone. This is a companion to a color shot which won a top prize in *Popular Photography's* contest some time ago.

I also find that water is a wonderful setting for the nude. When the girl is lying in the surf, for example, there is an interplay of the continually changing forms of the water and the resting female form that is the height of sensuous harmony. Water droplets on the skin are another delightful detail.

There is an enduring, timeless quality about a successful nude. I am constantly reminded of this by the continuing popularity of my book, *Figure Studies,* which is now out in a new edition with color plates added. It isn't only the absence of costume that keeps them from becoming dated. There is something about the nude figure in a natural setting that strikes a responsive chord in every human heart, no matter how sophisticated or overgrown with inhibition.

VIRGIN ISLANDS. The nude, such a "dangerous" subject in America and Europe, seems to come as a natural part of the surroundings in the solitude of the Caribbean. $^1/_{125}$ *second, f/22.*

Portrait Rapport

One of the tests of a competent photographer should be his ability to make a good portrait. Every working pro is called on at some time to take "head-shots"; even the industrial photographer who spends most of his time with machinery should be prepared to take portraits of company executives. And the amateur most of all ought to find continuing inspiration and challenge in photographing the human face.

In my earlier book, *Photography for Everyone,* I titled a chapter, "Portraits that Look Like People." I was objecting to those that *don't* look like people: the stilted poses of many commercial studios; the unmerciful direct-flash "police line-up" shot; and the hurried, thoughtless picture in which the subject simply looks uncomfortable and out of place.

Much depends on the way you approach portraiture. In some languages there are two words which are both translated in English as "face." One means "the face as an arbitrary arrangement of eyes, nose, mouth, etc." The other means "the face as a reflection of the personality or the spirit." When you grasp the difference between the two, you will be able to go beyond the passport and mugshot product and make portraits that "look like people."

From this you can guess that I think the most important element in portraiture is the relationship between you and your subject. If it isn't right, no amount of technical perfection can make you a good portraitist. This doesn't mean that the better you know a subject, the better your pictures of him will be. That would imply that your portraits of your mother or your wife would always be your best.

Sometimes it is possible to establish a rapport in a few moments that will be as effective *for photographic purposes* as lifelong acquaintance. You must instantly make it clear that you are not an adversary of your subject; that, on the contrary, you are his representative to the world through the portrait you are taking.

If the subject is a woman, she should understand that you see her as beautiful (or intelligent, or warm), and that your pictures will show her that way. If it is a man, the quality may be virility, strength of character, alertness. I don't suggest that you say these things to the subject in so many words; the particular method of communication is a highly personal thing. Often an exchange of seemingly irrelevant conversation, or simply an admiring smile, can do much toward establishing rapport.

Paradoxically, it is possible to know someone *too well* to make a good portrait of him—that is, without taking special pains. If a wife or girl friend has a large nose or prominent jaw, we tend to minimize it in our appraisal of her, and neglect the techniques that would flatter her. (In general, don't point large features toward the camera; do bring the camera in closer on features that need emphasis.)

I find that the twin-lens reflex is less intimidating to portrait subjects than the eye-level camera, especially when the sitter is shy. Perhaps it is because of the indirect communication at the moment of exposure. But there has been plenty of *direct* communication before that moment. This is again a very personal matter, but, as I have said before, I think the twin-lens is a "relaxed" camera; it creates less tension between photographer and subject—except for the desirable kind of tension generated by any serious work.

The picture of Betsy Lee shown on page 41 should remind you of the importance of lighting. In portraiture is is particularly noticeable and needs careful thought. In this case I used backlight from the sun, which is always beautiful with blond girls or children. Exposure, of course, must be for the shadow areas, not for the rimlight.

EMIL PREETORIUS. Here is the wonderful "character landscape" of maturity, the clear look into the distance. By a window in a bright room; Tele-Rollei with Rolleinar 1, 1/30 second, about f/14.

Page 34:
GEORGES BRAQUE, founder, with Picasso, of Cubism — in his Paris studio. 1/60 second, f/11.

Page 35:
BRAQUE AT HIS WORKTABLE. Sunlight, 1/50 second, f/16.

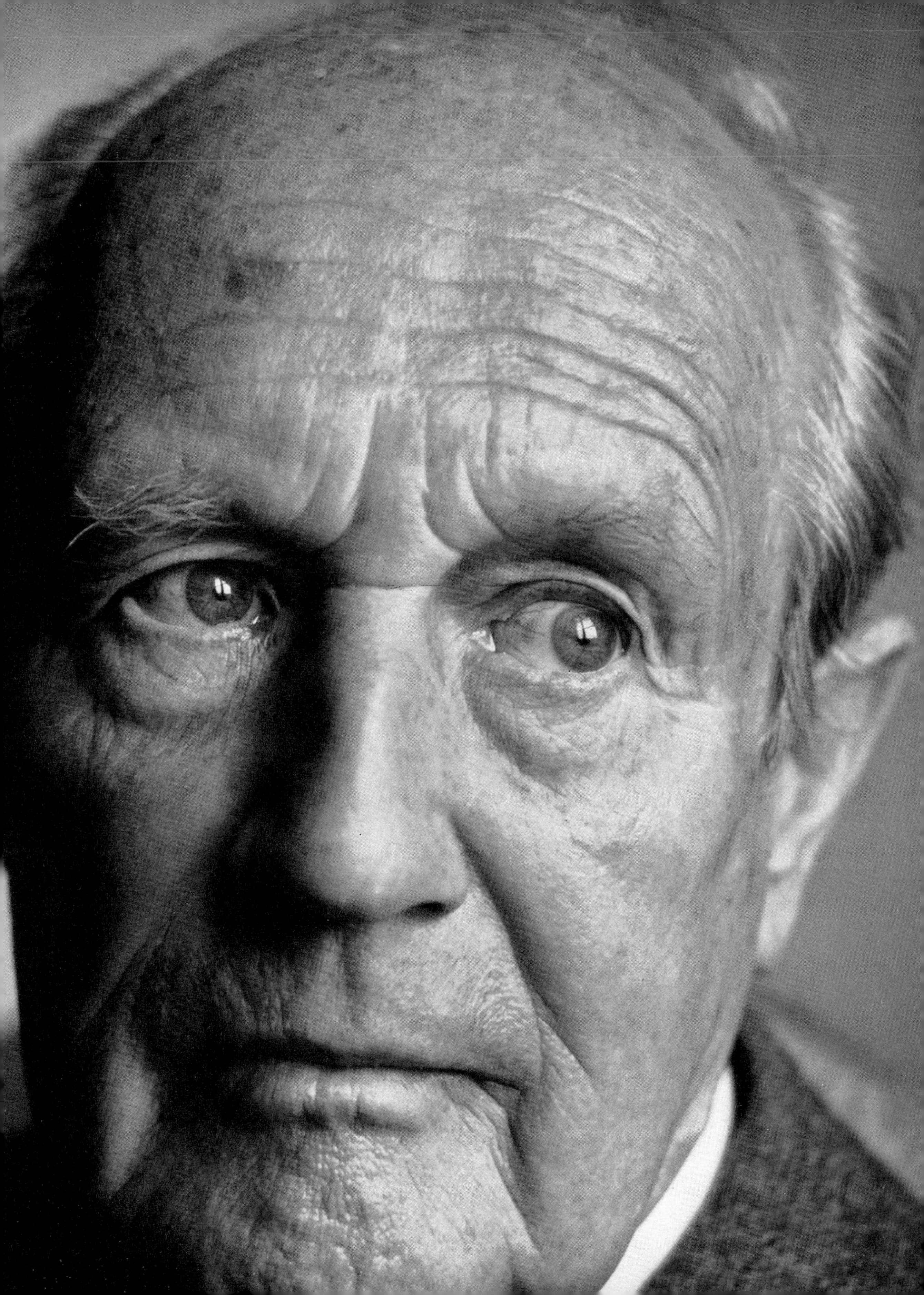

TWO MEXICAN PAINTERS: Left, Diego Rivera; right, José Clemente Orozco. Both photographed in full daylight, with no attempt at beautification. Orozco stood in the shadow of a church he was decorating with frescoes. The close-up was with Rolleinar 1, 1/25 second, f/8.

Page 38-39:
TWO CARIBBEAN HEADS: Left, an old native of Tobago; right, Geoffrey Holder, the famed dancer and painter from Trinidad, playing the voodoo drum.

GIRL ON THE BEACH. The American model Betsy Lee poses on the beach at St. Croix. I gave plenty of space to the background — sea, sky, air, and clouds — so that the portrait grew into a form in the landscape. To suggest youth, brightness, and freshness, I used infrared film, a dark-red filter, and a tripod (because of the slow shutter speed required), 1/8 second, f/11.

The "Different" Portrait

Strictly speaking, a portrait is a "pictorial representation of a person." Can it be more? Should it be more? Can we treat a human subject—especially a face—as we would an inanimate subject? Is it possible to photograph a face so that the picture contains more than a mere literal reproduction of its particular arrangement of features?

A passport photograph, or a three-for-a-quarter photomatic shot, is a pictorial representation of a face. But usually it bears little similarity to the real person who sat for it. One might say that these pictures would suffice for identifying a body in the morgue, but they give little clue to what the subject is really like—in personality, tastes, occupation, or surroundings.

We sometimes suffer from the urge to "get everything into" a picture—to include details that detract more than they add. Sometimes in portraiture we include or even emphasize aspects that are unflattering, and make a pretty girl look plain, or a plain girl downright homely.

There is nothing wrong with using a little imagination to make a portrait different. If you maneuver the model from sun into shade, or take an unusual angle, or include a prop to suggest the subject's interest of occupation, you are almost guaranteed a result that is far out of the "passport" class.

This imagination serves not only to get good portraits of plain subjects (as I suggested above), but to make even the most beautiful model look more alive and expressive. This was the case with my model in the straw hat. I was photographing her in direct sunlight, and it was no accident that we chose the straw hat that let through little slits of sunlight. A very slight turn of her head would completely change the pattern of light and shadow on her face. This was the most successful exposure.

The whole picture becomes an organization of forms—in addition to being a picture of a girl's face. You could sketch it in a few strokes of a pencil: the concentric ovals of hat and face, the curve of the blouse, and the counterpointing diagonal of the hat's shadow. So it is a portrait *plus*. In addition to the pleasure of looking at a pretty set of features, we have the pleasure of contemplating a well-organized unity. It is this *extra* attribute that turns a portrait into the kind of successful picture that gets published in picture annuals or eye-catching advertisements. But more important, it gives you the warm feeling of having made something more and better than just a "face picture."

The extra isn't always the play of light and shadow on the face. The portraits of Arnold Newman are instantly identifiable by the way they use the natural setting of the subject to evoke the whole personality. Other photographers have their own favorite ways of making portraits that are different. I don't suggest that every photographer should develop a trademark; it's better to approach each portrait on its own individual terms and see what can be done to make it distinctive.

Some of the most memorable portraits have been made with the most natural and easily available props, the model's own hands: I can think of many Karsh portraits; of the late Dan Weiner's strong picture of Judge Learned Hand; of Halsman's dynamic shot of Steichen pounding the table top. In my own work, I can remember many cases when hands contributed much to portraits. Hands can get in the way too, but your judgment and common sense will help you see when they are obtrusive.

FADO SINGER in Lisbon. They are a trio: vocalist, accompanist, and instrument. I had to make a corresponding "visual trio," and kept my hand on the focusing knob for complete control of the planes of sharpness.

GIRL IN STRAW HAT. The picture below is straightforward; but of course I saw immediately what the possibilities were with the straw hat — and Bliss Southerland beneath it. One of the possibilities is shown at right: a turn, an inclination of the head, and the hat becomes a shadow-creator, a pattern-maker, a frame, a protection, and a concealment. Now Miss Southerland looks out from a protective shadow. Eyes and earring glisten, skin turns silky, and there is a magical animation of surfaces. With the Rolleinar on the Tele-Rollei, my lens was almost under the rim of the hat. I was content: I didn't have just smooth teeth in a smooth face, but "the question" in a beautiful woman's eyes.

TWO CONTINENTS, ONE WORLD. Below, the Mexican beauty Nievis, model for many artists. She was lying on palm leaves, with one masking her face. She was looking upward, so the bright sky is in her eyes. At right, a dancer with the Royal Danish Ballet — the austere, reserved climate of the North, tempered by the eyes; behind her stood the "midnight sun" of a dazzling spotlight.

Men at Work

One of the things I do for a living is industrial photography, and one of the aspects I like best is the human one—men on their jobs. The pictures range from full-frame portraits of individuals to groups of workers pulling together at a task. Much of this photography is done outdoors, frequently in the semi-tropics, where the sun is fiercely bright.

A problem that often arises, naturally, is the excessive contrast of such light which might (for example) burn down on the bodies of a group of men but leave their clustered faces in deep shadow. This calls for some kind of fill-in. I always resist using flash for fill when it can possibly be avoided; it inevitably kills some of the naturalness of the illumination. And I don't carry any reflective surfaces—unless I happen to be wearing a white shirt—since I don't have an assistant to hold them for me.

The solution, then, is to take advantage of natural reflectors: water, a road or paved area, a boat deck, maps or plans on a table. I was able to do this with some success in the picture of the watchmaker.

Fill-in light is always important when you photograph a face in shadow—as you should to avoid harsh shadows and squints. The shadow doesn't always come from turning the subject away from the sun; in one of my favorite industrial portraits the face is covered by the long shadow of a cap bill; in that case, the fill was from a white-painted wall. This matter of daylight exposure, by the way, is one of the most taken-for-granted things in photography. My own way of working in bright light is, I realize, quite different from the general practice, and perhaps I should give an example of it. First of all, my standard black-and-white film—for everything—is Tri-X. I rate it at 200, disregarding the experience that leads others to use it at much higher ratings.

As long as the sun is brilliant, I keep an orange or deep-yellow filter on my lens at all times. In a great many of my shots the sky is very important, and the filter darkens it. Even if there are no clouds, any highlighted part of the subject stands out strongly against it. I allow a factor of 4 for this filter.

My standard exposure, then, is $^1/_{250}$ second at f/22. Remember that this is only when the sun is at its brightest and there is water or other reflecting surface around me. If there is less brilliance, I go to $^1/_{125}$ second. Experience—and there is nothing like it as a teacher—enables me to get such consistent exposure that my contact sheets can nearly always be printed without remaking for "overs" and "unders."

One other lesson I might pass along from my industrial experience. I have sometimes wondered—and even asked—why I get the nod for a job when I know a client has several other good photographers available. Very often it comes down to the fact that my shots are better organized, that people are in a more meaningful relation to their tools and surroundings; in effect, my composition is better. I am never conscious of this as I shoot, but I did have early training in the subject, and am aware of it when I look at pictures—mine or others. I would urge that every photographer expose himself to some art training. Esthetics can pay off, not only in dollars, but in satisfaction.

OIL WORKERS. It's hard work, the day was stormy, and for me it was an assignment (for Cities Service). Something down below wasn't going just right, and as the three oil-smeared men concentrated on a single spot, I shot — at 1/125 second.

PRECISION WORK. Below, the laboratory of the Cities Service Refinery in Lake Charles, La. What will be proved in the apparatus in the foreground is being worked out on paper in the background. I used f/22 for maximum depth of field, and a little fill-in light to balance with the outdoor light. Right, watchmaker in Biel, Switzerland: utter concentration on the work at hand; I, too, purposely "forgot" the background by using wide aperture. Close-up Rolleinar, small electronic flash unit.

Dogs, Cats, et cetera

Said Don Quixote: "Those who play with cats must expect to be scratched." No doubt; but they may also hope to get some fine pictures—between scratches. Before we go any further, let's include dogs, too, and any other pets of roughly the same size. This is another specialty for which the twin-lens is admirably suited. Remember that we said it was ideal for children, because the natural shooting position puts the lens below our eye level? The same is true for pets; whereas a 35-mm camera limits you to Gulliver's-eye views (unless you sit or lie down), the twin-lens comes nearer to the pet's "living level."

If you've had both a dog and a cat, you know how different are their natures. A dog needs people and relates very closely to them. A cat doesn't; it is completely independent and merely tolerates humans. For picture-taking, this means that you may have trouble keeping a friendly dog far enough away to stay in focus; or a cat may simply turn its back on you the moment you're ready to press the shutter.

Aside from these general traits, individual animals have their own characteristics, and the best pictures of them always come after a close study of those little attributes that set your pet apart from all others. Study the way they react toward other animals and to people, both owners and strangers. Consider whether you need or want to include a person in the pet's picture.

This brings up the general consideration of what other elements should be in the photograph. If you'll try to remember the strongest pet pictures you've ever seen, you'll realize that nearly always the animal has the stage to itself, with perhaps one other strong pictorial element, like a doghouse or a catnip pole.

It is particularly important to avoid distracting elements in foreground or background. A picket fence or a clump of bushes can overwhelm a small pet much more than it would a human subject. And when it is necessary to have a person holding the animal or coaxing it to pose or stay in position, try to have the person withdraw before you shoot. Nothing is more distressing than part of an arm or leg intruding on a pet picture.

On the other hand, if you intentionally include a human—particularly a child—you may get an even more appealing shot, but you're also taking a greater chance of failure. You have two subjects, and there is the problem of getting both of them just right in a single picture. Believe me, you'll be tempted to cut the best of each from different prints and make a composite!

A good answer to the background problem is to shoot against the sky, as I did in the shot reproduced here. In this case I feel that the pyramid of the hands holding the cat contributes rather than detracts from the composition. A medium-yellow filter is advisable to bring out clouds in such a situation.

In winter, you may be doing much of your pet photography indoors, and wherever available light isn't sufficient, I would recommend bounced electronic flash. In addition to being more convenient than floods, it permits you to stop action—which can make for a special kind of fine pet shot. I think of a cat's motion as like an arrow's: a dog's more like a bouncing ball. Watch a cat at the moment of its spring: there is a leopardlike tension in the muscles, then the explosive action, aimed like a missile.

When a dog jumps for a stick, for example, every part of the motion seems to anticipate the next. As he leaps upward, he's already prepared to land; and when he lands he wastes no time getting off the ground again. You can anticipate both of these kinds of motion—though you may have more trouble getting the *exact instant* with the cat. Pets in action (or pets at rest, for that matter) are a specialty in which you must be prepared to shoot roll after roll of film before you become proficient.

FOOT RACE: Poodles are clever. He knows his friend Maria very well, and leads her gently by the leash. Here I didn't want to interfere, so I used the Tele-Rollei, and for the rapid action shot at 1/250 second.

PLAYMATES. Below, the same pair as in the previous picture, now at rest, and still close friends. They are brightly lighted by reflection from a white wall. Tele-Rollei, yellow filter, 1/60 second at f/16. Right: On Dad's boat with his pet cat; same data as picture opposite.

Animals around You

There has been much interest in what I've written about photographing animals with the TLR, so it many be a good idea to talk about the subject again.

It seems to me that two fundamental mistakes in approach prevail in taking pictures of pets or other domesticated animals. (I rule out wildlife for the moment as a completely different problem.) Curiously enough, some people tend to think of a dog or a cat, when it is before the lens, as an inanimate object, like a statue or a bowl of fruit, which only has to be arranged and lighted properly for a good picture.

On the other hand, some amateur photographers who are especially fond of their pets can't help feeling that the animal is really just another human being that is somehow "different." In all candor, I think that no matter how well you have trained a pet and achieved an "understanding" with it, it shouldn't be photographed as though it were human.

There is one detail, however, in which the photographing of animals is like taking pictures of children. When I wrote about the latter subject, I suggested that a parent or other close adult should be present—to attend to the model while you attend to your camera and what you see through it.

This applies to animals, too, and for the same reasons. (For "parent or close relative," read "owner or master.") A dog requires stimuli to keep him looking alert and changing expression, and when your nose is buried in the groundglass, you're not the most diverting dog-entertainer.

Cats, of course, cannot be distracted from their own train of thought for more than a second or two at a time. You must usually enter into their world to get a good picture, whereas a dog can easily be induced to enter yours.

I like to photograph all animals outdoors, under conditions as favorable as possible. Because of the likelihood of unexpected motion in the subject, shutter speed should be kept as fast as lighting will permit. For me, this usually means 1/250, sometimes 1/500. I don't mind opening the aperture to *f*/5.6 or *f*/4 if necessary (rather than going to a slower shutter), because the important part of my subject is in a fairly shallow plane and I usually don't need to keep foreground or background sharp if the object is simply to portray the pet.

Soft lighting may not be quite as bright as direct sun, but I find it preferable for animal pictures. Under strong light squinting is a reaction as prevalent in pets as in people. And with dogs, I find less tendency to prolonged, slack-tongued panting in shade than in sun. A slightly overcast day (which is hard to come by in my Caribbean shooting-grounds) or open shade exposed to a bright sky is nearest to ideal.

The profile of the white poodle here was made with backlighting—particularly good for putting a "halo" around light-furred animals. Exposure is a particular problem with this technique. A meter reading must be taken close up, so the instrument isn't overinfluenced by the backlight. If the animal's coat is light, *don't* be generous with exposure, or the fur will lose much of its texture. The converse is true with dark fur, though error is less often objectionable.

By the way, this shot illustrates one of the ways direct sun can be used without unfortunate results: when it is behind the subject.

With color, deviations from precise exposure are even more noticeable. I feel that, again, it is most vital to avoid overexposure. If experience—with the meter or the judging eye itself—has not yet brought you dependable perfection in exposure, I strongly advise bracketing shots. As you know by now, film is cheap!

SPANISH SHEPHERD. He loved his sheep and had several aboard his donkey. In the background, the town of Avila on a rainy day. Yellow filter, 1/250 second, f/5.6.

Page 58:
OUR POODLE. You meet him here for the third time, but in our private life he is much more frequently seen. He is a thoroughbred, and to show his breeding he arranged the profile and backlighting himself. Rollei, 1/250 second, f/11.

Page 59:
YOUNG DEER. I like fawns so much because they seem to be made of porcelain. Tele-Rollei, 1/250 second, f/11.

Helicopters and Other Birds

As our increasingly air-conscious population is finding out, even the most familiar terrain looks entirely different from overhead. I suppose every amateur photographer who has ever been in a plane has taken pictures from one—and the results haven't always been gratifying.

In a commercial airliner, there are factors working against successful pictures: unfavorable seating, reflections (and even dirt) on windows, and above all, an altitude that usually makes things on the ground seem disappointingly far away when you look at the contact prints. Generally, the best pictures from airliners are those that include some part of the plane and a beautiful cloud formation or sunset.

Naturally, the best "sky hook" for your camera is a private plane—one that is being piloted for your own picture-taking convenience. And best of all is a helicopter, which can make the slightest of movements to get you into precisely the shooting position you want.

In fact, the helicopter is the only "tool" for aerials that permits you to get composition just as you want it, without endless circling and reflying. A skillful pilot like Don Rogers, who flies me over the various paradises of the Virgin Islands, will react to the slightest motion of my hand to help me get just what I need.

The 'copter's slow speed and ability to "stand still" in the air don't permit me to reduce my shutter speed. Because of the craft's vibration, I always shoot at 1/500 second on Tri-X film. The aperture is standard at *f*/11 for most subjects; if there is a lot of bright reflection, I go to *f*/16. These settings allow for use of a medium-yellow filter, which I use here (as almost all the time) because there is generally some sky—often with clouds—in my aerial shots.

Focusing is never a problem: the camera remains set at infinity all the time. And here, as I find myself repeating for so many situations, the groundglass of the twin-lens is ideal for framing aerials. It is reassuring to see the elements of the composition fall into place just as they will look in the finished print.

Of course, when we talk about shooting from a helicopter, we're not discussing something inexpensive and easy. Provided you can find a helicopter-plus-pilot for hire in your area, it will cost at least $65 an hour; I haven't paid less than $100 in the Caribbean. Small single-engined conventional aircraft are a good deal less costly, and you can shoot very well from them if you can sit by an open window. I have made some excellent pictures from Apaches, Cessnas, and the like.

If there is Plexiglas between you and the outside world, it can cause reflections that may completely kill your pictures. But even if you can't open the window, it's possible to reduce chances of reflection by getting the lens as close as possible to the glass without touching it. (If it touches any part of the plane, the added vibration will make the camera hard to handle.)

In propeller-driven planes, I often use the sportsfinder, particularly when the altitude is low and the ground is going by at top speed. True, I sacrifice the groundglass viewing, but the use of the $2^1/_4 \times 2^1/_4$ camera is still justified because of the larger image size. When subjects are distant, you want all the detail and enlargeability you can get.

As for color, I use Professional Ektachrome, which works nicely with the shutter speed remaining at 1/500, and aperture at *f*/8 for normal subjects, *f*/11 when there is mostly white beach or silvery water with high reflectivity in the picture.

OLD CITADEL in Haiti, a landmark from a romantic past, was photographed from a Haitian Air Force fighter plane on a particularly rough flight. A shutter speed of 1/500 second was none too fast under the circumstances.

Two on One

There used to be a story about a photographer who built a successful and prosperous career on a mistake—an unintentional double exposure that looked more creative than anything he had done before. All he did was to switch to *intentional* double exposures! It sounds more like a legend to me, but it's true that, in the days when few cameras had double-exposure prevention, pros did get a lot of kidding when they goofed. And it's certainly true that beautiful pictures can be made by the intentional and careful use of double-exposure technique.

Today almost all twin-lens reflexes have double-exposure prevention, but many manufacturers have provided for the photographer's experimental urge by adding a release mechanism to "prevent the prevention." The twin-lens is exceptionally well suited to making on-purpose double exposures, because it is one of the few compact camera types with an accessible, full-size groundglass.

This is important because you will often want to reference marks on the glass, to help you get the second image just where you want it in relation to the first. You may even want to sketch in all the forms roughly in advance, if it is a picture that can be completely planned before shooting.

Since I used the word "experimental" in connection with double exposures, let me make a distinction between the "fooling around" that passes for experimentation among many amateurs, and the careful, deliberate use of known techniques to get a particular kind of result. You're welcome to snap blindly in all directions and call a lucky result "experimental" if you like, but I'm talking about the other kind.

I think the most successful and interesting double exposures are those thas show a subject as the eye might see it in two successive glances. When you make a portrait that combines profile and full-face views, you may succeed in showing more of the personality than either of the views could do alone. The principle applies to almost any subject. I say "you may succeed" because it is unbelievably easy to fail, to combine two images in such a way that they simply confuse each other.

My own favorite pictures of this type are a group of nudes, of which one is reproduced here, and some images of New York's lights which I made soon after the end of the war, combining double exposure with camera movement. The latter took special planning, and I used the groundglass as a kind of miniature planning board, sketching in the lines with light strokes of a grease pencil. These marks are easily removed, especially in a camera whose focusing hood is removable.

THE BIG SHADOW. This is a double exposure; the large "shadow" was made first, then the realistic nude, at different distances. Both exposures were at 1/30 second, f/11.

Outdoor "Still Lifes"

There is a kind of picture which I suppose could be called a landscape, but which depends for its success not on the appeal of fields and trees and mountains, but on a relationship between the elements that is immediately satisfying to the eye. The elements—the subject matter—may be very humble: the weathered siding of an old building, a rock, a tree stump, an expanse of grass. The point is that the subject, for itself, may be nothing—but the arrangement is everything. That is why I have titled this page to suggest a similarity with studio still lifes.

As with the controlled indoor situation, the key to success is selection and simplification. When you set up a still life, it is relatively easy to refrain from adding elements that are unnecessary. But, for example, in a city scene there are so many things that clamor for inclusion that it is difficult to avoid confusion, distraction, and chaos.

One primary difficulty is the failure of the photographer to see all that will be in his picture. He is so preoccupied with a dominant feature or a central object that he doesn't notice an intruding foreground or a cluttered background or another element that will prove to be as dominant in the finished picture as the desired subject. Learning to see in this way is a laborious process for many people, and most of the learning is from one's own mistakes.

Another problem is the failure to previsualize depth of field. You may want to play one element against another for balance, not realizing that one of the elements is much farther from the camera than the other and will be out of focus on the film. This is of course more of a problem at wide apertures, and so is most often encountered in bad weather or other poor-light situations. When shooting at *f*-stops wider than *f*/8, it is always advisable to consult the camera's built-in depth-of-field scale.

A similar problem arises when there is atmospheric haze or fog between you and the more distant parts of your picture. The eye tends to see into such haze more easily than the film does. When your subject has elements in the near, middle, and far distances, they may be separated by the fog into three distinct planes.

This leads into the central problem of these "outdoor still lifes"—the spatial relationships between parts of the picture. When you are making such a picture, try to visualize what a change of shooting position would do. Notice how a change of only a few inches can make it an entirely different picture. This is a clear case in which I feel the twin-lens groundglass makes composition easier.

THE PALM LEAF, on Paradise Island in the Bahamas. The palm leaf fills the empty space and emphasizes the loneliness and abandonment.

Page 66:
QUIET IN THE UNQUIET WATER. White highlights dance on the blue-black water; where is the diver who has just plunged in? Tele-Rollei, Ektachrome Professional, 1/125 second, f/16.

Page 67:
NEW MEXICO DESERT. Here the rule of the empty foreground is broken. Should the agave plant have been in the foreground, like the palm leaf two pages back? No, here the monotone of the sand "waves" becomes a subject in itself; insignificance becomes significance. The desert is empty. This is one of my most frequently published pictures. Rollei, 1/125 second, f/22.

Camera . . . Action!

Stopping rapid motion is a common problem to photographers lacking considerable experience. But it is one of the techniques which the TLR simplifies to the point where anyone can become proficient in a short time.

I like to think that following a moving subject on the groundglass is like watching a movie or a television screen, once you have learned instinctively to keep the camera moving smoothly with the action. And you watch it *continuously*, without any break at the instant of exposure.

Most TLRs today have maximum shutter speeds of 1/500 second, which, if used properly, is fast enough to stop an automobile moving across the line of vision if it is not too near or really speeding. This brings up the subject of the direction of movement relative to the camera's angle. It's easy to understand that if a subject is advancing directly toward the camera (or going away from it), its motion will be much easier to arrest than that of a subject crossing at right angles to the camera's axis. But how much easier? Well, for example, a person walking leisurely toward or away from the camera can be pretty well stopped at 1/25 or 1/30 second. But the same figure, walking at the same speed *across* the camera axis, would require about 1/100 second to stop.

These figures are roughly doubled and quadrupled, respectively, for subjects like a bicycle rider and a moderately rapid automobile. As you might except, when the action moves at a diagonal to the camera axis, you can split the difference: a car coming from 45 degrees would need about 1/250 second.

These are all approximate figures for *stopping* action, to get reasonably sharp images. This is the way I prefer to work, although others feel that intentional blurring of the motion contributes a feeling of the activity.

As a rough guide to the degree of blur at various speeds, let's picture a girl running fast, three or four yards from the camera, right across the field of view. At 1/500, she can be virtually immobilized with both feet off the ground. At 1/250, the image will still be sharp enough to satisfy anyone but a fanatic, with just a bit of blur at the extremities. At 1/125, you will see the result that blur lovers most often strive for. At 1/60 or 1/50, there are no more hard lines in the subject, and at 1/10 or 1/8 there is not even a complete form, but only an unrecognizable suggestion of what might be there.

The picture of water skiers shown here involved more than consideration of shutter speed. To begin with, I have established that in bright sun on water, using Tri-X at a conservative rating and a medium-yellow filter, I can advance my shutter speed to its maximum of 1/500, close my aperture to the almost-minimum of f/16, and get a good exposure. This is what I did for the skiers.

Most water skiers, until they are quite experienced, ride at some distance from the towboat—farther than you imagine, until you've seen them from the boat. So it's good to be able to extend your focal length. I used the Tele-Rollei with its 135-mm lens to pull in the two skiers. What I wanted was the towboatman's-eye view, which dwarfs the skiers in relation to the wake kicked up by the speeding boat. For a closer shot, I would have worked from another boat or gone out with an accomplished skier who could safely work on a short tow.

WATER SLALOM. The water skiers are in St. Croix. I used the Tele-Rollei to bring them within range, and because of the fast action I shot at 1/500 second, f/16, with a yellow filter.

Focus is another consideration; in action situations you should always be prefocused. Unless you can anticipate the camera-to-subject distance, set the scale at the hyperfocal distance (that is, the point at which everything from *half* that distance to infinity will be sharp). With the 135-mm, it happened to be about 25 feet; with the normal 80-mm, it would be about 15 feet.

Tips for Bad-Weather Shooting

I'd like to pass along a few tips about shooting with the twin-lens under adverse weather conditions. Some believe that the smaller the camera is, the easier it must be to use in rain or snow. Not necessarily so; a 35-mm which must be raised to the eye for each shot is bound to be exposed more to the elements than a twin-lens that can be operated quite easily in the semi-protection of a raincoat or overcoat.

My way of working in inclement weather is to keep the camera open, ready to shoot, under my raincoat or topcoat, with the buttons fastened over it. (Never mind how it looks; sometimes the amusement of the prospective subject will make a picture easier to get!) The lens shade—always an indispensable accessory—is always in position to keep precipitation off the taking lens. The focusing hood, of course, is open, and if the light is especially poor, the magnifier is also in position to help with focusing.

If you have a coat with pocket-slits to reach inside pockets, you can focus and advance film without exposing more than the two lenses as you shoot. You can sight down through the groundglass right inside the coat. With the combination of your body and the coat as protection, you can shoot in any direction except into the wind without getting moisture into the camera mechanism. (Let me inject here: if you do get moisture on the camera, wipe it off thoroughly. If you suspect some has gotten inside, take it to a repairman for a check-up before using it again.)

Since light is generally weaker in bad weather (except in snow), use a fast film. I have standardized on one of the high-speed films for virtually all black-and-white work, even in bright sunlight, and with close collaboration with my processing lab I have no trouble in getting fine-grain results.

Color film can give you some pleasant surprises in bad weather. Ektachrome will usually need to be exposed on a tripod when skies are overcast, but the results can be gratifying, though they may not exactly reproduce the colors in the scene as you remember them, since this film is balanced for sunlight. Super Anscochrome will permit hand-held shooting, since it is more than three times as fast, and will give quite different color renditions from Ektachrome. I would particularly suggest using color when a setting sun is visible through the clouds, when there are bright foreground colors to set off against the somber background, and of course, when there is a possibility of a rainbow.

If you have trouble seeing the image in the groundglass because of poor light, probably your camera does not have a device for brightening the picture. You can have one installed under the groundglass of any $2^1/_4 \times 2^1/_4$ camera at little cost. On the Rolleiflex the built-in feature is called Rolleiclear; one of the accessory ones is called the Hartley field lens.

You have a certain psychological advantage in bad-weather photography. In most people's minds there is still the idea that sunshine is required for picture-taking, and when they see you with a camera they think, "Poor dope, he doesn't know any better," and they don't stiffen before your lens as they would in bright daylight. This suggests a whole area of photography: people's reactions to adverse weather. You might try standing at the entrance of a public building and shooting people as they emerge into snow or rain, grimacing and pulling up collars, fumbling with umbrellas in the wind, etc.

But what I would most like to emphasize about bad weather is the *quality* of the light. There is something indefinable, yet tangible, in the light just before a thundershower, or in the light reflected from wet surface after rain, or in the glow of a gray sky on snow. It is the ability of film to capture these subtleties that makes it so worthwhile to brave the elements for the challenge they offer.

RAINY DAY IN SARDINIA. The rain brought the boys into step — under a sufficiently large umbrella! 1/125 second, f/11.

Pages 72-73:
PUDDLES. These two reflections are pages from a sketchbook. They are only suggestions, yet they speak out what is significant. They have the stimulation of fragments; the incomplete is completed by the viewer. Left, the Gothic weight of Cologne Cathedral; right, the southern baroque of Munich's Theatiner Church. Both made at about 1/60 second, f/16.

HURRICANE ON TOBAGO. The elemental force of the wind, itself invisible, is here made forcibly apparent. In the middle of the rain, I shot through the windshield of my car. 1/125 second, f/11.

Working with Subjects in Depth

As I have mentioned before, here and in other books, one of the most troublesome shortcomings of inexperienced photographers is the inability to see *everything* in their picture—not only in every corner of the square format, but also in every plane of the three-dimensional scene that is reduced to two dimensions on the groundglass.

Once you have learned to either eliminate or harmonize the nonessential parts of your subject before you shoot, you will find a new freedom in searching for pictures.

We have discussed composition and mentioned the use of foreground objects to frame a subject. These matters are closely related to my present topic, yet different. So far, we have thought of these parts of the picture as they appear on the flat surface of the groundglass. Now I would like to consider objects that are so different from the main subject in camera-to-subject distance that they don't seem to be part of the picture you see through the viewing lens.

Single-lens reflexes offer you the opportunity of looking through a stopped-down lens, so that in theory you can preview depth relationships as they will be in the final picture. But in practice, when you stop down to the usual daylight apertures, the image becomes so dim that you are no longer sure just how much is sharp. (This, like most matters that affect camera preference, is a subjective opinion; obviously there are many photographers who don't find this true in their way of working.)

As a twin-lens user, you have grown used to seeing only a shallow plane of sharpness at each setting of the focusing scale—shallower as you reduce the distance. Consequently, if you are not thoughtful, it is easy for you to assume that what looks like a white blob on the groundglass will be an unobtrusive white blob in your picture. At *f*/16, this won't be the case. The blob will become a very sharp area of sun glare, or a poster with distracting lettering, or some other disturbing element.

So you must see the subject clearly first with the naked eye, taking account of *all* the planes in it, before turning to the groundglass. And until you have made depth-of-field judgment a part of your automatic technique, refer regularly to the depth-of-field scale. It will tell you, for instance, that at *f*/8, when you focus on 15 feet, your area of sharpness extends from about 10½ feet to 23 feet. And you can use the camera as a rangefinder to see just which parts of your picture fall within those limits.

The picture made in Hamburg harbor has been chosen to show how a number of planes can be interrelated when sharpness is not left to chance. Perhaps it is too simple an example, since it was shot with lens almost completely stopped down. With experience, problems like this solve themselves automatically, but if I had been shooting "by the numbers," I would have reasoned something like this: I want a lot of depth, and I am using a fast film, so I can stop down. My meter says I can go to *f*/16 at the desired shutter speed. I set my focusing knob so the infinity mark is opposite *f*/16 on one side of the depth-of-field scale. Then opposite *f*/16 on the other side of the scale I see 11½ feet.

Next, I focus the camera at 11½ feet and approach the nearest part of my subject, to make sure that I don't get any closer than that distance. Then I refocus at about 23 feet—the setting at which everything from 11½ feet to infinity will be sharp. Thus I am sure that everything in my finder will be sharp, even though only one plane *looks* sharp at a given moment.

The same technique works equally well when you want part of the picture *unsharp*. Simply make sure the desired area is outside the zone of focus. But whatever you do, make sure you get what you think you're getting!

CARIBBEAN SCHOONERS. I made it a game to frame the distant ship precisely in the chains, lines, and sail of the schooner in the foreground.

BRANDENBURG GATE. The atrocity of barbed wire is here a foreground political symbol — before an older symbol of tradition-rich validity. Between foreground and background is not a distance of a few yards, but the cleft between two worlds. Wide-Angle Rollei, yellow filter, 1/60 second, f/16.

Page 78:
HAMBURG HARBOR. Another example of framing with a nautical subject. Yellow filter, 1/125 second, f/22.

Page 79:
CASTLE OF THE PRINCE OF WALES at Carnarvon. The nautical flavor is suitably British. The anchor as framing foreground emphasizes the stark, simple architecture.

ACHTUNG

PERCHED BY THE SEA. This was a color picture which, partly because of the massive frame in the foreground, works out well in black-and-white.

TEMPLE OF THESEUS in Athens. The Corinthian capital in the foreground brings strength, tension, and ancient detail to the picture. Behind the crisply sharp foreground, beyond the ruins, stands a vision: the temple of a god, landmark of a lost world. Yellow filter, 1/5 second, f/22.

Big, Square Color

I have been debating whether it's possible to write about color as it applies to the twin-lens reflex, and as you can see, I've decided it is. Sure, color film is color film, no matter what its size, but there are a few specific points to be made. And anyway, it gives me a chance to unload some of my ideas about color in general.

The twin-lens is ideal for color, I feel, because it is a compromise between the heavy, slow-moving 4×5 and the miniature that makes eye-straining 1×1½-inch slides. The 2¼×2¼ format is the smallest that can comfortably be seen without magnification by most people. My clients—like your friends and relatives—find it perfectly simple to see a transparency and decide whether they like it by holding it up against a light source.

Since cost is important to many people, especially in color film, I ought to remind you of the false economy of miniature film. A 36-exposure load tends to make people shoot faster and with less thought and care than a 12-exposure one. Of course you can take "nothing" pictures on the shorter roll too, but the tendency is to take greater pains. I'll bet if we could measure such things, we'd find that the average amateur gets about the same number of good pictures per roll, whether it has 12 exposures or three times as many. So don't think only of per-frame cost.

It has always seemed to me that our square format makes the framing of a picture even more important; that is, the introduction of some foreground element that "holds in" the center of interest. In color, this works out in a lot of interesting ways. Looking back over some of my published color pictures, I see instances where I have used bright yellow coral and sunlighted leaves in the foreground of a sea and skyscape to balance the intense blue. In another set, where I was posing a blonde girl against a pale blue sky, I wanted a frame that would not overpower the delicate skin tones, so I put her behind a massive piece of neutral gray driftwood.

Even though some of my most successful color shots have been those with the strongest primary colors—like those of the Caribbean carnivals—I insist that color doesn't have to scream to be good. I am always pleased to find a situation in which the colors are muted or subdued, and some of my personal favorites are shots in which perhaps only a single pale color predominates.

An argument I sometimes hear against 120 size for color is that not many projectors will take it, and after all that is the only way to show transparencies to a group. True, there aren't many such because so many users are satisfied with viewing them unenlarged. Rollei makes an excellent one, and there are a few others. You should check with your camera store if this argument has been holding you back. Also, there is a least one excellent table viewer which takes both 120 and 35-mm slides, projecting an image about a foot square, and folding into a compact, flat case.

In my studio I have a continuous exhibition of my color pictures, usually mounted in glass with metal frames on a specially built light box against a wall. It permits visitors to see several dozen pictures at a time without squinting, and it's a great help to me in sorting and organizing my new work. It is a relatively simple device involving fluorescent tubes, a sheet of opal glass, and wooden cross-strips spaced about 2½ inches apart. If you're handy, you can easily build a similar one; even having it made to order won't cost very much, and you'll find it an ideal way to keep your color off the shelf and out where people can look at it and enjoy it.

BOETTCHERSTRASSE, BREMEN This color picture has been compared with paintings by Lyonel Feininger. People have either admired it or reproached me, claiming that it is no longer real photography. As for technique, it was simply shot through textured stained glass, on Ektachrome, 1/15 second, f/22.

Kodacolor—and Related Matters

My choice of materials is dictated to some extent by my clients' preferences; this is especially true in color. Advertising agencies generally prefer to work from dye transfers, particularly when the originals are $2^1/_4 \times 2^1/_4$. I have always been happy (and have satisfied my customers) with Ektachrome and (recently) Professional Ektachrome.

Professionals have tended to regard Kodacolor as an amateur's snapshot film—as it was in fact intended to be by the manufacturer. Now, with its print material perfected and many labs trained to use it to perfection, there is beginning to be more widespread use of the negative color for professional applications.

Since I don't have time to experiment very much, I hadn't used Kodacolor extensively until a couple of years ago. I began by shooting it alongside Ektachrome when it was convenient, and for some personal pictures that I'd never need in dye transfer.

The results were gratifying, and I was especially pleased with the quality of the black-and-whites made from it on Panalure paper. This is the remarkable material made specifically for use with Kodacolor negatives, compensating for the contrast-reducing and exposure-increasing effect of the orange masking layer. Prints can be made on conventional paper, too, but they will tend to be flat and require painfully long exposures.)

Shooting these color pictures for myself, without the pressure or demands of an assignment, made me think again of the amateur's most common problems with color. As a pro, I solve most of these problems without thinking—or else they don't arise.

One of the chief difficulties is failure to take into account factors which increase the intensity of light—you might call them "light magnifiers." They are, for example, a white sand beach, a water surface, an expanse of light-colored wall, or a stretch of clean concrete pavement.

If you have memorized a standard bright-sunlight exposure, and use it when there is a bright reflecting surface around the subject, you are almost certain to be overexposed—perhaps by a stop or more. If you depend on a meter you may have just the opposite problem. If any of that bright surface is allowed to influence the meter, you will be distinctly underexposed. So take readings only from very close distances. My illustration is a case in point: if I had used the "bright-sun" recommendation of $^1/_{50}$ at *f*/11, all the highlight detail would have disappeared. Not wanting the building in the background to be any sharper, I doubled the shutter speed instead of closing down the aperture.

Another fault I have noticed in two ways: in amateurs' pictures, and in the way they approach their subjects. (I see a great many Caribbean tourists with cameras.) This fault is "too-many-yards-between-lens-and-subject." A person's face may be the only center of interest, yet it is only a half inch high on the transparency or negative. I would suggest the rule, "Always get at close as you can unless there is a good reason not to." Of course this doesn't apply to landscapes or large group shots.

Why mention it in connection with color? Because unfortunately most amateur color never gets cropped. With black-and-white you can push the enlarger to the top of its column and get the head as big as you want it (although with loss of quality). With color it is always advisable to get the image you want, *and no more,* on the groundglass before exposure.

ROME FROM MT. PINCIO. This "simple" color photograph without any dominant subject breathes the air of the South, under the serenity of the Roman sky. Tele-Rollei, Kodacolor, sunset.

A Tripod? Yes, When You Can

Nobody likes to carry any more equipment than his picture-taking needs will require. I suppose the most overburdened photographers are the amateurs who fear that the gadget they leave at home is precisely the one they will need most—and consequently carry all the equipment they own on every Sunday afternoon shooting expedition.

A professional soon learns to anticipate his needs accurately, and to know what he can leave behind when approaching a particular assignment. I have found that there is a certain irreducible minimum of items that I must carry almost everywhere, and one of them is a tripod. There is just no excuse for unsharp pictures resulting from camera movement, and I frequently find that I must use a shutter speed so slow that some perceptible camera motion is almost unavoidable.

Of course the ideal choice is the lightest tripod that still provides really stable support, and that is the kind that always travels with me.

Now that I have made an airtight case for tripods, let me face a question that unforunately still arises in many places around the world. What do you do when the use of a tripod is forbidden for one reason or another? There are many public places, in the U.S. as well as abroad, where a tripod or accessory lighting equipment makes you appear commercial or (in the opinion of authorities) obstructs the traffic. In a crowded museum, for example, the latter may really be true. Sometimes, though, I think the authorities simply do not want professional competition with "official" photographers who make the "authorized" views of tourist attractions.

In Greece, tripods are not permitted in the shooting of many classical antiquities. There I frequently found that the combination of my conservative film-speed rating, a small aperture for depth of field, and a filter requires me shoot at $^1/_{15}$ or $^1/_8$ second. Bracing the camera on a wall or other solid support is fine, but those solid supports seldom seem to be where I'd like them.

The only solution, of course, is to make my body as much like a tripod as I can. This means a firm but relaxed stance, such as rifleshots use, and as perfect a union as possible between camera and body. I use a neckstrap, shortened to bring the camera very close to my eye, and keep my elbows in close to the body.

The picture opposite shows a situation in which utmost depth of field was needed; the stone pillar in the foreground was only seven feet away, and I wanted to keep the temple ruins sharp in the distance. Stopping all the way down to *f*/22, and figuring the filter factor for a deep-yellow filter, I found that I had to shoot at $^1/_8$ second.

For the desired angle, I dropped to one knee and braced the camera on the other. In any such unfamiliar position, you have to be careful that you are not under strain or likely to fall out of balance.

Of course, I would take advantage of a wall or other upright surface to lean against. Two legs plus a motionless vertical object make an almost perfect tripod, and often such a wall or post can be used in this way even when it is not feasible to brace the camera directly against it.

Apart from the example in the illustration, the most obvious situations requiring firm camera support are those in which light is poor, so that even a reasonably wide aperture calls for a slow shutter. In addition, my personal preference is to avoid extremely wide apertures, and try to make the various planes in the scene work together, rather than throwing them out of focus.

There are other substitutes for a tripod: unipods and "chest-pods." I presume these are exempt from tripod bans in restricted places, although I have not tested this. Most "chest-pods" would require adaptation for use with the twin-lens.

RUINS OF CORINTH. The proportion and scale of the ancient world, destroyed for thousands of years, yet indestructible, are still expressed through photographic perspective. No tripod, but carefully held (see text); $^1/_8$ second, f/22.

NEW YORK AT NIGHT. Rhapsody in black-and-white . . . painting with light. Only the picture below shows the night-lighted RCA Building as the tourist sees it. All the others are the product of fantasy and technique, not visible until the finished picture. They include carefully planned combinations of double exposure and camera movement. The camera was on the pan-head of a tripod, and with the shutter open, it was moved in vertical, horizontal, or diagonal directions for a total of about 60 seconds (at f/5.6). The groundglass served as a kind of miniature "drawing board" on which the exact position of the blurred second exposure could be superimposed upon the sharp first exposure.

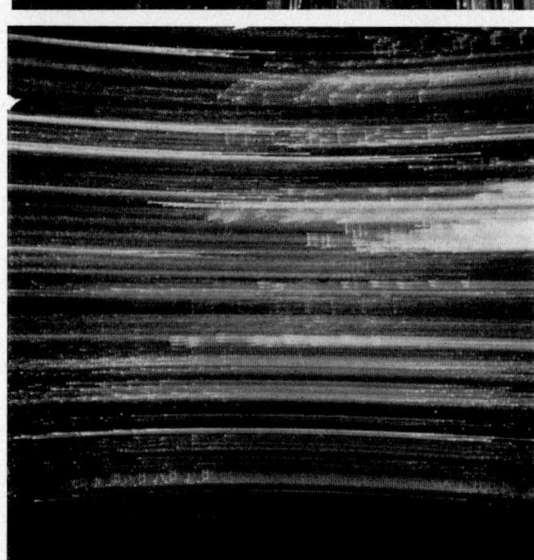

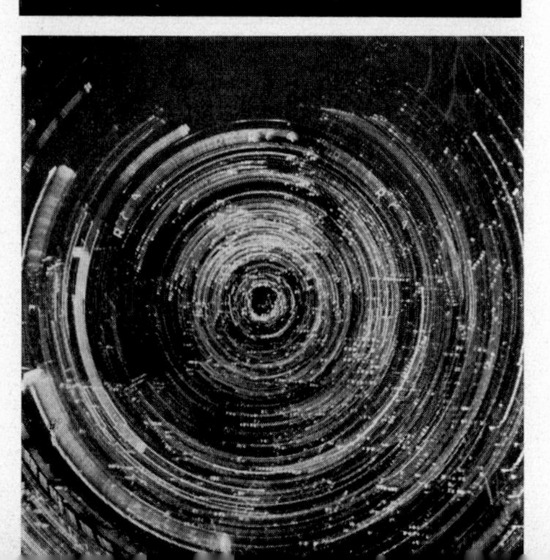

RCA

Landscapes: Top, Middle, and Bottom

The first photograph ever taken, I'm told, was a still life. I'd guess the second was probably a landscape. "Natural scenery," as the dictionary defines it, has always been one of the most popular camera subjects. There are some special considerations in making good landscapes with the twin-lens reflex.

First, the groundglass offers what I like to think of as a "three-dimensional contact print" showing what the eventual picture will look like. As I move around and change camera angle, I can see the picture organizing itself in a much more normal way (for me) than I could in an optical viewfinder.

It is characteristic of landscape to be not only horizontal, but broadly so. How do you handle an essentially horizontal subject in a square format? A simple but wasteful way is to ignore the upper and lower parts of the square, and crop later to a horizontal. But why not turn the square format into a distinct advantage, and use every bit of it? In nearly every landscape situation, while you may be looking only at the center of interest, there are things going on in all parts of the picture area. If there is no predominant background, like mountains, consider clouds. Learn how to use filters that make even a wisp of cloud look dramatic in a dark sky. Even when there are no clouds at all, an orange or red filter can turn an empty sky into a massive dark area that may fit the mood of your picture perfectly.

Often it is even more important to look at what is right under your nose. Foregrounds can be used creatively in several ways. If there is a graceful tree branch, it can be used to frame the scene. Look also for such things as a wooden fence, low foliage, and human or animal figures than can be introduced to lend interest to the picture.

If these foreground elements are to frame the subject in the traditional way, they should be sharp, and this will mean you must use a small aperture. In a landscape, the most distant areas must generally be sharp, so the camera should be focused at infinity, and the *f*-stop determined by consulting the depth-of-field scale for the aperture which will keep the nearest elements in focus.

Another way of using the foreground is increasingly popular today: using out-of-focus objects or areas as masses of tone (or color) to set off the center of interest. You might even have both foreground and background unsharp — but the question arises whether the picture would still be a landscape.

If a sky is totally blank, or a foreground completely without interest, it can be largely excluded by concentrating on the opposite area. That is, if you do not want to use the sky, take special pains to see that the foreground makes a real contribution to the composition—or vice versa. I have made some pictures that are almost "cloudscapes" because the dramatic sky so completely dominates them. In others, interest is divided between the middle distance and some action in the foreground, while the sky is only a narrow strip at the top.

But the principle is the same always: try to use *all* of the square. Remember that any cropping requires a greater degree of enlargement, and thus some loss of quality. More important: your camera has a square format, not only by accident, but because that format has been tried for over three decades and a great many photographers have found it ideal.

So begin thinking of landscapes not as wide horizontal sweeps of scenery, but as pictures that can be put together harmoniously in normal rectangles, with plenty of room for dramatic skies and interesting foregrounds framing the subject.

"FUJISAN," THE HOLY MOUNTAIN. Finally Pearl Harbor and Hiroshima are past, and holy Fujisan rises in undisturbed majesty. (Foreigners call it Fujiyama.) Rollei 4×4, 1/125 second, f/16.

Page 92:
LAKE LANDSCAPE, GERMANY. The magic of reflections helps to convey the actual experience. Yellow filter, 1/250 second, f/22.

Page 93:
TRIMARAN, a lightning-fast boat, was caught at 1/500 second, f/16. I wrapped up the foreground in seamanlike fashion.

Pages 94-95:
STRAITS OF GIBRALTAR. In the foreground is the Spanish coast, in the background the African, under a brightening sky after a rainstorm. Tele-Rollei, 1/60 second, f/16.

Page 96:
TOLEDO before an oncoming storm. A photographic repetition of the famous El Greco painting, from exactly the same viewpoint. Yellow filter, 1/125 second, f/22.

Page 97:
ST. EUSTATIUS, near the Antilles island of St. Kitts. Seen and photographed from an airplane, even the most familiar landscape becomes quite different. Yellow filter, 1/500 second, f/11.

Put It in a Frame

Traditionally, the framing of a painting has been a necessary final step, a recognition of merit, a kind of "setting for the jewel." Now we seldom use frames on photographs, but we can often improve them by putting frames *in* them.

When you look into the groundglass, your field is cut off by its limits; this is one kind of frame, dictated by the camera's format. But there are infinite possibilities for using framing elements in the subject itself for stronger pictures.

If the subject is distant, as in a landscape, you can add an appropriate feeling of depth and perspective by including something in the foreground which frames it. You might step back into the doorway of a barn so the dark silhouette of it forms a frame. Or you might find a convenient tree with an outstretched branch which could frame the view on two sides.

Architectural subjects especially lend themselves to framing. They are sometimes cold and matter-of-fact, and a surrounding foreground makes them more appealing.

Two of the examples shown here were made in Florence, Italy, and show two kinds of framing. The magnificent buildings of Florence have been so often—and so well—photographed that I searched many times for ways of making my pictures different. In both of these, I combined two aspects of the city's architecture in a single image, for example framing the graceful tower of the Palazzo Vecchio in a quatrefoil of stonework in the Campanile of Giotto.

I am reminded of a picture I took in Wyoming several years ago, which people still remember today—partly because it won a prize in *Popular Photography*'s picture contest. It was a color shot of a ranch in the montains; the ranch was so far away that it would almost have been lost without a kind of frame to direct the eye. There was a split-rail fence nearby, and I placed my camera so it ran diagonally across the lower part of the picture, and the ranch was framed between two of the big X-shapes of the fence supports.

Here I was primarily trying to get some foreground interest, and discovered that at the same time I could use the fence for framing. It isn't necessary to encompass the subject on all four sides.

This leads me to a very important technical question: Do you want the foreground frame to be as sharp as the rest of the picture, or would a certain degree of unsharpness aid by making the frame less distracting? If you decide everything must be sharp, you must select an aperture small enough for the required depth of field. Your camera has a scale indicating depth at any given aperture, either in the form of a plate attached to the body or viewing hood, or incorporated with the focusing scale on the lens mount.

Very often, especially with color film or when light is poor, your small aperture will demand such a slow shutter speed that hand-holding the camera is not advisable. A tripod or some other solid support is a must. Individuals vary in their ability to hold a camera steady; some claim they can shoot at 1/5 or even 1/2 second, while others insist that movement shows up in their pictures if they hand-hold at speeds slower than 1/100. Practice will certainly improve your steadiness, and it's worth the trouble. We have come some distance from the subject of framing, but this is a good example of the way *seeing* pictures is always tied up with technique. I feel it is important to *decide* things like sharpness or unsharpness and not let them happen accidentally. It is equally important to command the techniques that get the effects you want.

BREMEN CATHEDRAL is reflected in the windows of an old house. I like this kind of photographic "window-peeking," as also in the picture of the Berlin Gedaechtniskirche two pages further on, and especially that of Boettcherstrasse in color. It presents an opportunity for heightening experience, for a kind of "refraction" of cold reality. And the window frames make wonderful frames for pictures!

Below:
VENICE CAMPANILE photographed through the legs of the famous horses of St. Mark's. 1/60 second, f/22.

Right:
MEMORIAL CHURCH in Berlin is seen both through the open window (left) and reflected in the glass (right). The destroyed past is thus optically set beside the sober present, which is enveloped in a light like organ music. 1/60 second, f/22.

Pages 102-103:
FLORENTINE ROSETTES. Two shots from the Campanile in Florence: left, toward the Palazzo Vecchio; right, toward the cupola of the Duomo. Giotto, like many architects elsewhere, provided the photographer with the most beautiful frames for his subjects. 1/125 and 1/30 second, respectively, at f/22.

When Is a Subject "Ready"?

One of the hardest things to agree upon about a picture is whether it was taken at just the right time, and contains all the elements it should have, but no more. This has to be subjective. I might like a serene, rather empty landscape, and you would prefer to have people or animals in it. Again, you might insist on getting the peak of an action, and I might prefer the moment leading up to it or the moment showing its result.

But at least we can understand the things that make a picture different at varying times and under different conditions, and so get the picture we want more often.

Suppose you are out for a walk with a camera, wanting pictures of whatever kind you encounter. You look into the groundglass from time to time, and when you like what you see, you take a picture. Now, what is it that determines whether you shoot or not? (Let's omit action shooting for the moment; the urgency of the split second usually dominates all other considerations of "when.")

Even in the quietest landscape, you cause a change in the relationships of things as you move through and around it. New elements spring up in the foreground to heighten an effect of depth; trees or buildings seem to move closer or farther apart. These space relationships change like the image in a kaleidoscope—one moment adding up to nothing, the next moment making a harmonious picture. Try a few dry runs like this, watching the picture on the groundglass rather than the scene as the eye ordinarily takes it in.

This enables you to visualize in terms of the finished picture, whereas looking at the scene directly you may not get such a sense of space relationships. I have written about framing, and that is one of the elements that change as you move with the camera. But there is also the placing of a foreground figure in relation to a scene, or the relating of two or more other important elements.

Light is another vitally important element in determining when to shoot. It can also force you to change your own location or position when it is unfavorable. One of the most frustrating conditions to some amateurs is a sunny day with windborne clouds moving rapidly in front of the sun; just when they think they have the perfect picture in direct sun, a cloud obscures it and they get a badly underexposed shot with the dramatic effect totally lacking.

It does take alertness to see-and-shoot before the picture is lost. But you can learn to judge the amount of time between clouds and when to expect the sun to emerge. This reminds me of a case where scattered clouds can contribute to the very best pictures. In vast landscapes, where there is difficulty in separating the planes to give a sense of depth, the patches of bright sun can act like spotlights, picking out particular areas as they pass over the scene.

If you pose a child in bright sun and see that it is making him squint, you know that isn't the time to press the button. If the sun strikes an old stone wall from the front so you can't see its texture, you know it's better to wait until the light strikes from the side—perhaps earlier or later in the day.

In photographing places, it is always important to study them in advance, so an unexpected condition won't spoil the picture at the time go to take it. This is partly why so many travel pictures are inferior; they must be made on the run without any preparation.

NET-THROWER, HAWAII. The wind, surf, sky, strength, and grace — all coming directly toward the photographer. 1/500 *second.*

Page 106:
BEAUTY OF ST. LUCIA, or, Temptation at the Harbor. Evening, 1/125 *second, f/11.*

Page 107:
"FOUNTAIN" IN THE GULF OF MEXICO. This is the geyser caused by an underwater explosion aimed at detecting oil deposits beneath the sea. Wide-Angle Rollei, 1/500 *second, f/16.*

Watch the Light !

It is common for amateurs (and a few pros, I'm afraid) to discover their errors only when they see prints of their pictures. Dr. Edwin Land has made it possible for many of them to correct their mistakes ten seconds after they are made. But we who use cameras other than the Polaroid can have it better still—if we are clever enough. We can spot trouble before the moment of exposure, and do something about it.

Since a photograph is made solely by light, it isn't surprising that many of the mistakes you might make are mistakes with light. Let's forget about artifical light and consider only sunlight in its various forms.

The sun, being the ultimate source of all energy, is a mighty formidable piece of lighting equipment, and ought to be used with great care. When it is full and strong, and you are surrounded with areas of high reflectivity (as on the beach), you will be driven to your highest shutter speeds and smallest apertures to get proper exposure with some films. This is fine for both motion-stopping and depth of field—but naturally the techniques of selective focus and action blur will be out of your reach, for the most part.

There are two companion problems with direct-sun shooting: squinting eyes, and jet-black shadows cast by eyebrows and noses. The former is the most disturbing, but you can sometimes catch a laughing expression so that it looks like a squint of merriment rather than of sun blindness. As for the shadows, I have sometimes deliberately permitted them, where I felt a face was strong enough, or the shadows added to its strength. But the best pictures of people in direct sun are made with backlight. This means in effect that the subject is providing his own shadow, by turning his back to the sun. Your exposure will be longer, of course. Be sure to take a meter reading close up or (for incident-light meters) with the cell shielded from the sun. Anything in the background that is receiving sunlight will be drastically overexposed. With a woman or a child you will get a beautiful halo effect as the light spills through the hair.

So much for direct sun—which is after all the least desirable kind of daylight. Much to be preferred are two kinds of subdued sunlight: overcast and open shade.

When there is atmospheric haze and the sun still manages to come through enough to cast a shadow, some really beautiful effects are possible. The light is enough for modeling, but not enough to cause squinting or black facial shadows. This can also be a wonderful light for color, but the results are not predictable because of the wide variance in the parts of sunlight—its constituent colors—that are filtered out by the haze and smoke.

When the overcast is so thick that you can't make out the sun's position, you have a light source that is shadowless and especially flattering to the faces of women and children. But this is a very low-contrast situation, and you will have to take measures (like underexposure and overdevelopment) to keep your pictures from going too flat.

Open shade provides light from the sunlighted sky; it is generally brighter than overcast and gives more modeling and separation of tones. It is especially fine for color when the sun is really brilliant. And because the light is relatively strong, you can use the faster shutter speeds that enable you to catch children at play and other moving subjects.

You can teach yourself a lot about the different kinds of light by looking carefully at pictures in books and magazines, and thinking what kind of light you would use if you wanted to duplicate them.

WHITE WALLS OF RHODES. A silhouette, and the almost mathematical division of space into blacks and whites under the dazzling Aegean sun. Yellow filter, 1/250 second, f/16.

Above:
GYPSY DANCER, GRANADA. The dancer is lighted from the front by daylight through a door, and more strongly by a single lamp high behind her, placed there for this purpose. $^1/_{125}$ second, f/8.

Left:
TEXAS COWBOYS. An unexpected opportunity that required very fast reaction. This is one of my best-known oil-industry pictures. Backlight, $^1/_{500}$ second, f/11.

Twelve Are Enough

I contend that the 12-exposure film load of a twin-lens reflex is an actual advantage over those that hold three times as many frames. I'm tired of hearing that three dozen shots gives you three times as many chances for good pictures as one dozen. On the contrary, for some photographers—especially beginners—the long film load is like an invitation to bang away recklessly, and that's no way to approach picture-taking.

The twin-lens encourages you, almost forces you, to think while you shoot. Just as good art of all kinds is largely a matter of selection, of knowing what to leave out, so your percentage of fine photographs can be raised by learning to say *no* to your trigger finger.

If you're a twin-lens user by preference, one reason may be that you feel at home with a system that makes you think while shooting. I have an idea there may be such a thing as a "twin-lens temperament," as opposed perhaps to a "35-mm temperament." That would account for the very strong convictions of the partisans of both types. Naturally, thinking takes a little more time than not thinking, but I wouldn't imply that twin-lens photography is slow. I've always been able to shoot as fast as any situation demanded, and I can change film in just a few seconds with almost automatic movements.

The most rewarding moments in photography are those just before the instant of exposure, while the picture is coming into being. To me, it makes absolutely no sense to shoot before the picture is born, so to speak. The results won't be what you want, and you may miss the really valuable instant. That negative-size groundglass is like a stage on which the picture's elements arrange themselves or respond to your arranging. There is no better photographic eye-training than practicing to see pictures within that little square frame.

Never think of a roll as "only 12 pictures." Think instead of how many that is, and how wonderful it would be if you could capture 12 real pictures on 12 frames. Actually, what with the factors of inexperience, clumsiness, and plain bad luck, you're a good man if you succeed half the time.

Try some eye-education exercises. Pick a simple subject, something that's not going to run away or change form while you shoot, and study it in the groundglass from many angles and distances. Carefully make what you consider are the 12 best pictures of it. Bring the contact sheet back to the subject, and study the two together. Did you get what you thought you saw? Don't give up until you've made the picture you really wanted. Then move on to more complex situations, exploring each one clinically before making an exposure. By the time you've satisfied yourself with difficult subjects like a human face or a sports event, you'll have given yourself a full-scale course in seeing, and learned some visual lessons you'll never forget.

I don't want to give the impression here that I think other types of cameras are for people who work thoughtlessly or carelessly; nothing could be more absurd. Obviously you can think just as long and just as creatively behind one camera as another. What I'm talking about is something psychological, perhaps too subjective to apply generally. But it is a feeling evolved from many years of peering into that little square of glass.

Since I have spoken so far as though all twin-lens reflexes were limited to 12 exposures per roll, I had better hasten to mention the exceptions. Some manufacturers provide masks for making 16 horizontal pictures, for people who want to save one-third more on film. There are 35-mm adapter backs, indispensable if you prefer Kodachrome to films available in rolls. And the ultimate, probably, is Rollei's sheetfilm adapter to make pictures one at a time.

BULL IN PALACE OF KING MINOS (Cnossos, Crete; 3,500 years old). Colorful antiquity, even though marred by scrawls. Tripod, reflected daylight, Ektachrome Professional, 1 second, f/11.

ΠΑΡΘΕΝΙΑ
TANIT
TUNIS
19 62
VIC

Is Composition Old-Fashioned?

There are some words which are heard today almost exclusively in camera clubs, and found in books written more than 20 years ago. Some of them have justifiably fallen by the wayside, but some have simply dropped out of common usage because overwork has turned them into clichés. An example of the latter is composition.

Two kinds of critics helped to kill the meaning of composition. One said, "This picture is badly composed," and considered that the last word. The other launched into a complicated explanation that made composition sound like some kind of religion. No wonder that a lot of serious photographers today shun the word.

But they don't shun the thing itself—not the good ones. It is almost a hard-and-fast rule: *Any picture which deserves to be called "good" has good composition.* The only exception might be a news shot or other picture in which the subject matter or the moment of exposure are of overwhelming importance.

If you were asked to photograph a set of dishes in a studio, you wouldn't stack them all in the right half your picture area, or across the bottom of it; neither would you dump them at random from the carton and shoot them as they happened to fall. You would try to work out something *orderly, balanced,* and *pleasing* to your eye. By whatever name you called it, you'd be creating a composition. If you had some training in art, you might find it easier to arrive at a good arrangement, and you would be more confident of your success. But the untrained eye can often compose naturally, just as some people are naturally gifted with the drawing pencil.

When you are working in a live situation with your camera, the problem is not so different as it might seem. You are not moving inanimate objects around in a small space, but you have many ways of insuring the *order* and *balance* that will be *pleasing* to the eye. First of all, you must be aware of more than the central subject which first drew your attention. Often the surroundings will be part of your finished picture when you hadn't really noticed them during shooting. Or perhaps the surroundings are purposely excluded when they might have contributed to the picture.

The point is that good pictures are not made consistently by accident—even accident in small details. If you are shooting a pretty girl your first thought should be that the surroundings must not detract from her. But the more positive and equally important second thought is: How can the surroundings *add* to the picture? The same applies to any kind of subject—a building, a flower, a child, a dog. We have previously talked about *framing* the subject with part of its surroundings, and about using all parts of the square format so that nothing need be cropped. These are all aspects of composition.

One of the most difficult problems in composition is the picture in which there are several points of interest but no dominant or central subject.

As you can see, these principles are not easy to convey by words alone; ideally they should be taught by showing several pairs of pictures—a good one and a bad one in each situation. Perhaps you can teach yourself, to a degree, by careful study of your own prints. And don't be afraid of that unpopular word *composition!*

PARIS NIGHT CLUB. Because of the very low light level, I used the (for me) unusually wide aperture of f/4, and braced the camera for a 1/5-second exposure.

Wide-Angle and Tele Reflexes

Wide-angle and long-focus pictures have been possible with the twin-lens for some time, by the use of interchangeable or slip-on accessory lenses. Today both are possible with cameras expressly made for them—the Tele-Rolleiflex and the Wide-Angle Rollei. I find these two cameras so useful that I am never without them when I travel on assignment. They make it easy for me to get pictures I would never have attempted without them.

The Wide-Angle has a 55-mm Distagon *f*/4 lens, with a 71-degree angle of coverage (as compared with 56 degrees for the normal 75-mm lens). It produces no apparent distortion at all with most subject matter—though I suppose it might if there were straight lines at the extreme ends. I found it most useful in the Gulf of Mexico, for example, when I had to photograph the geysers caused by underwater oil-prospecting explosions. Being on a boat, I couldn't "step back" to get more in my picture. I wanted to get the prospectors' boat in the frame and the Wide-Angle got not only that but the sun backlighting the tip of the geyser. Result: a well-composed picture with an added fillip that made it a stopper.

This situation, by the way, is one that points up the two-dimensional nature of the Wide-Angle. It's not merely a panoramic camera; perhaps it should be called a "high-and-wide-angle." There is a temptation to think so much in terms of wide subject matter that you forget the lens is also seeing above and below your sweeping panorama. This could leave you with a blank sky and a surprisingly cluttered foreground. Sure, you can crop them out when you print. But it's so much better to think while you shoot and put something interesting in these areas.

The Tele-Rollei has a 135-mm Sonnar *f*/4 lens with a 33-degree angle of coverage. This brings the subject closer, so that you can shoot at greater distances (and remain unobtrusive) without making the image infinitesimal on the negative. So it is ideal for shooting people whose normal activity you don't want to disturb. I got some wonderful off-guard shots with the Tele on my last European trip.

Portraiture is perhaps the most useful application of a moderately long-focus lens. It avoids the distortion usually present when normal-length lenses are used at minimum focusing distances. But even more important, I think, is the psychological fact that a camera at five feet from the subject's face is a lot less inhibiting than one at three feet.

The Tele-Rollei itself focuses down only to about 8½ feet. But there are special Rolleinars designed for it: the 0.35 and the 0.7 (the figures referring to diopters). The former allows you to go to about 4½ feet, and the latter as close as 3 feet. Of course, at that minimum distance, you're getting into the inhibiting range again! The more powerful Rolleinar is not intended so much for portraits as for other close-up subjects. An editor asked me whether I follow the usual practice of prefocusing for a portrait, then moving forward and back to keep the subject in focus. Somehow this doesn't seem natural to me; I stand still and keep my fingers on the focusing knob if there is movement in the subject.

CASTLE OF CHILLON. *Here it swims, in the living mirror of Lake Geneva, in the green of the water and the green of the reflected forest slope. Tele-Rollei, Ektachrome Professional, 1/30 second, f/16.*

Can You Focus in the Dark?

It's a revelation to me to see how many people there are who have strong feelings about twin-lens reflexes, and who are eager to read about the special uses and problems of this type of camera.

Some people have mentioned the difficulty of focusing on the groundglass when light is poor, and asked whether anything can be done about it. I don't often face the problem myself, because when light is that poor I prefer to supplement it with flood or flash. However, there are some things that can be done to improve focusing in available light. First, you can install a field lens under the groundglass. This is a square piece of glass with concentric rings inscribed on it, and it has the effect of brightening the image at the center. The Rollei people make a refined version called the Rolleiclear, which has the additional virtue of narrowing the apparent depth of field, so that it's easier to tell when a given plane is in sharp focus.

Field lenses don't brighten the whole groundglass area evenly, so you have to pick an object near the center of the frame to focus on. And this suggests another general technique for poor-light focusing. Try to pick out an area of the subject which is sharply delineated and reflects more light than its surroundings. It might be a white shirt or the edge of a lamp shade. If this spot is in or near the important part of the picture, fine. If it isn't, focus on the bright object first, then swing around to frame the subject you want. But you'll have to be pretty good at judging whether the two planes are at the same distance from the camera!

One obvious way to solve the problem would be to throw a beam of light on the subject while focusing. I've known photographers to carry pocket flashlights for this purpose, but it seems to me rather clumsy and intrusive on the subject. There is a device made for press-type cameras which incorporates a light beam with the rangefinder, but so far as I know there is no such device available that can be adapted to the twin-lens reflex.

But I think I've gone too deeply into a problem that probably doesn't affect very many people. Most reflexes give a good bright image on the groundglass under all but dismal conditions, and I suspect there are photographers who are always trying to push their equipment beyond its capabilities, to make things exceedingly difficult for themselves. The obvious answer to insufficient light is: turn on another lamp, or take the girl to the park and forget the coal-cellar situations.

The photographer who likes to take candid pictures with flash, in places where there is little room illumination, has a related problem. I'd guess his trouble is not as serious as the available-light man's; the latter has to use a wide aperture, so his focusing becomes vastly more critical, while the flash man may be working at *f*/8 or *f*/11, which allows him considerable margin for error. And the further the subject is from the camera, of course, the less need for precise focus.

A reasonably well-developed eye for judging distance is handy in cases like this. But if you're still getting unsharp flash pictures, better confine such shooting to situations where distance is known or can be measured in advance.

On bright days you may get glare on the groundglass. Brother, that's a warning signal! Glare on the groundglass means flare on the film—and spoiled pictures. Stand so that your lenses are shaded somehow, by a tree or a person's shadow.

TAXCO CATHEDRAL, Mexico. Here there was bright daylight coming from above, but the overall light level was not high. I took a chance on a hand-held exposure at 1/5 second at f/5.6.

Left:
MEXICAN STORM. The Cathedral of Taxco stands out momentarily against lightning-brightened clouds. A night shot with tripod; exposure 1 minute at f/11.

Below:
PLACE DE LA CONCORDE. The Egyptian obelisk stands at the heart of the gleaming Paris night. About 30 seconds, f/16.

FRANS HALS MUSEUM in Haarlem, Holland. The day outside was rainy, and I photographed the two young critics under a skylight, using a tripod for a ½-second exposure at f/5.6.